MONSTER TRUCK COLORING BOOK

25 MONSTER TRUCKS YOUR KIDS WILL LOVE!

MICHAEL STEWART

CONTENTS

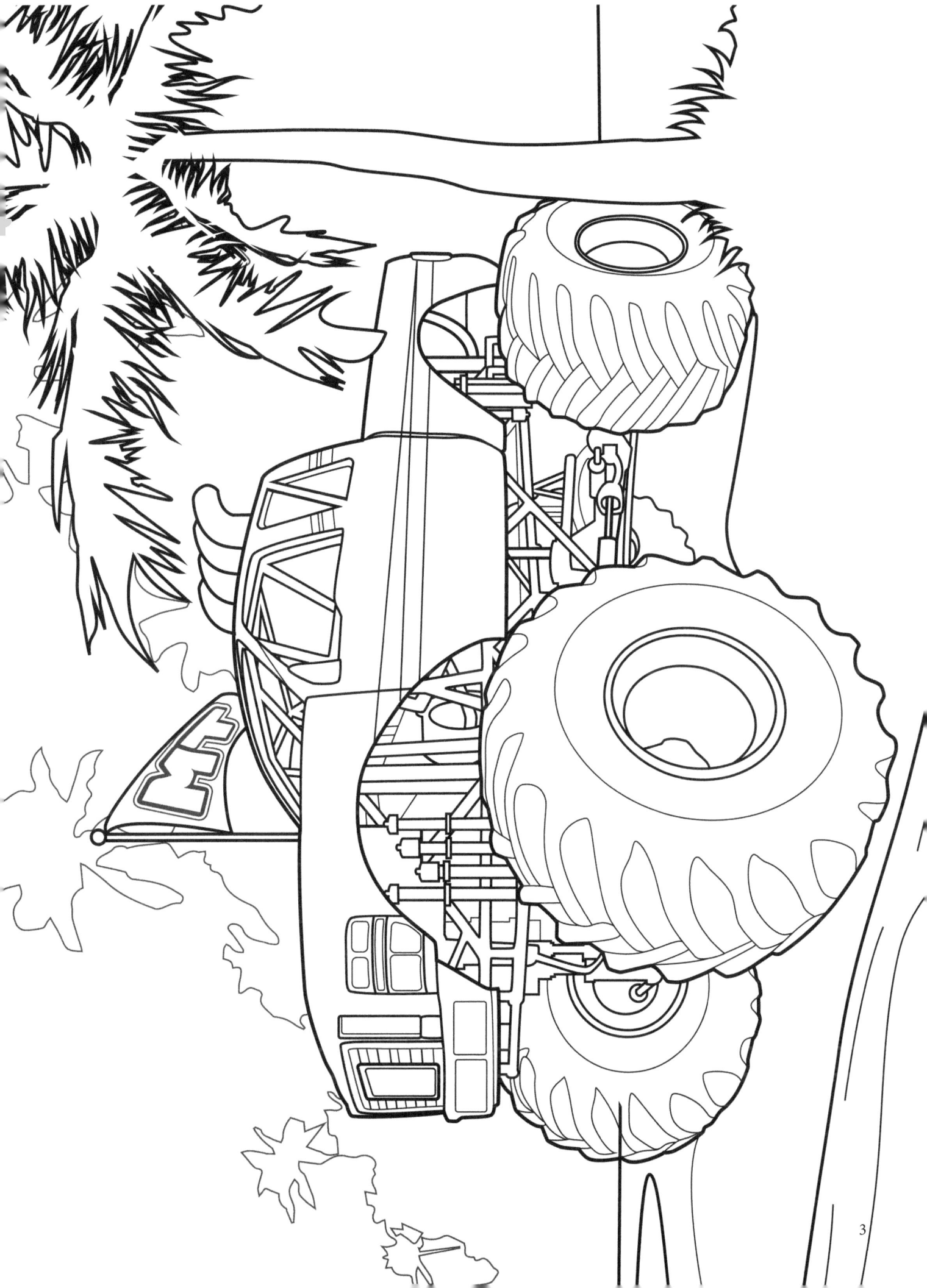

Plate 1.

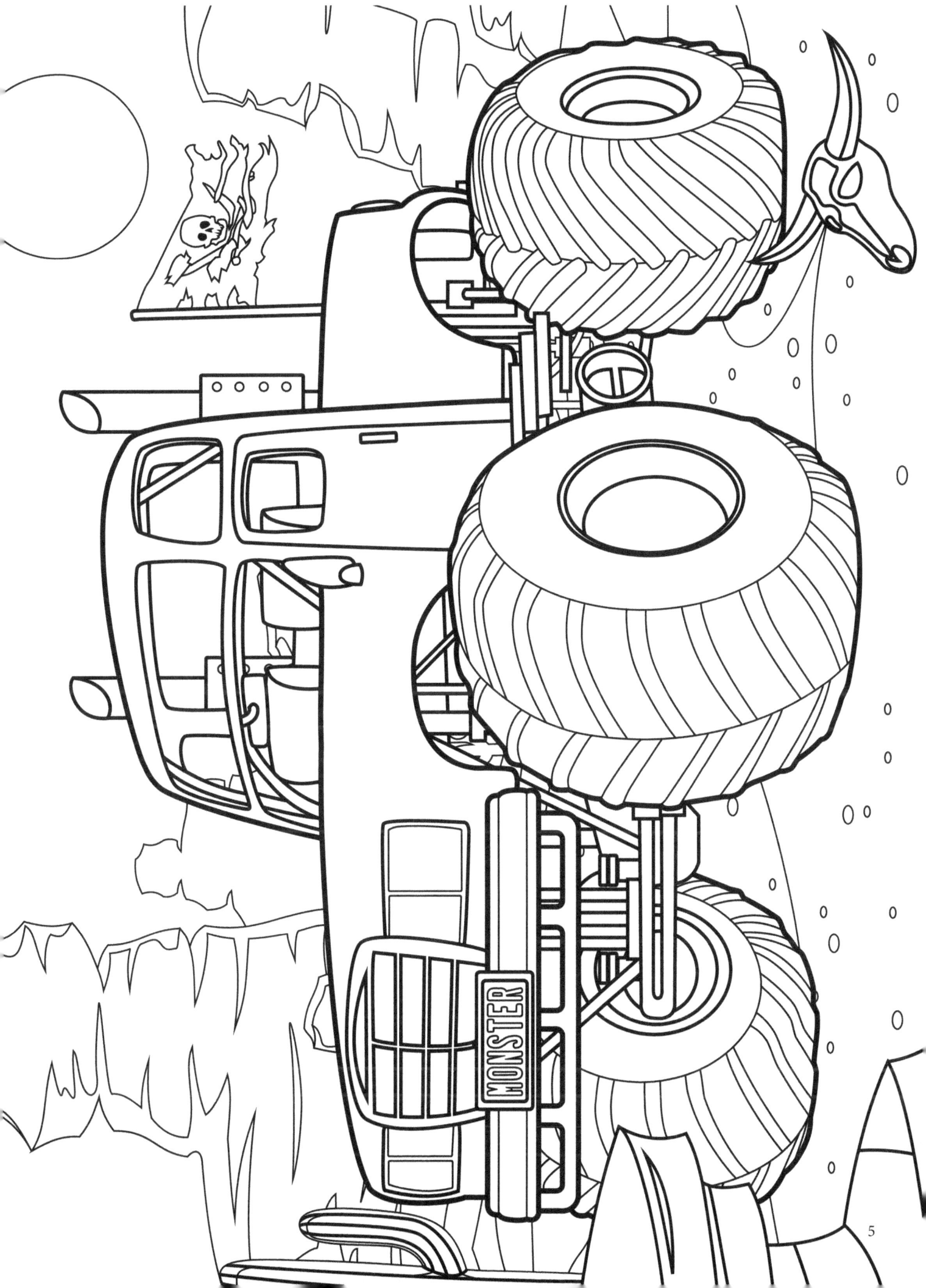

Plate 2.

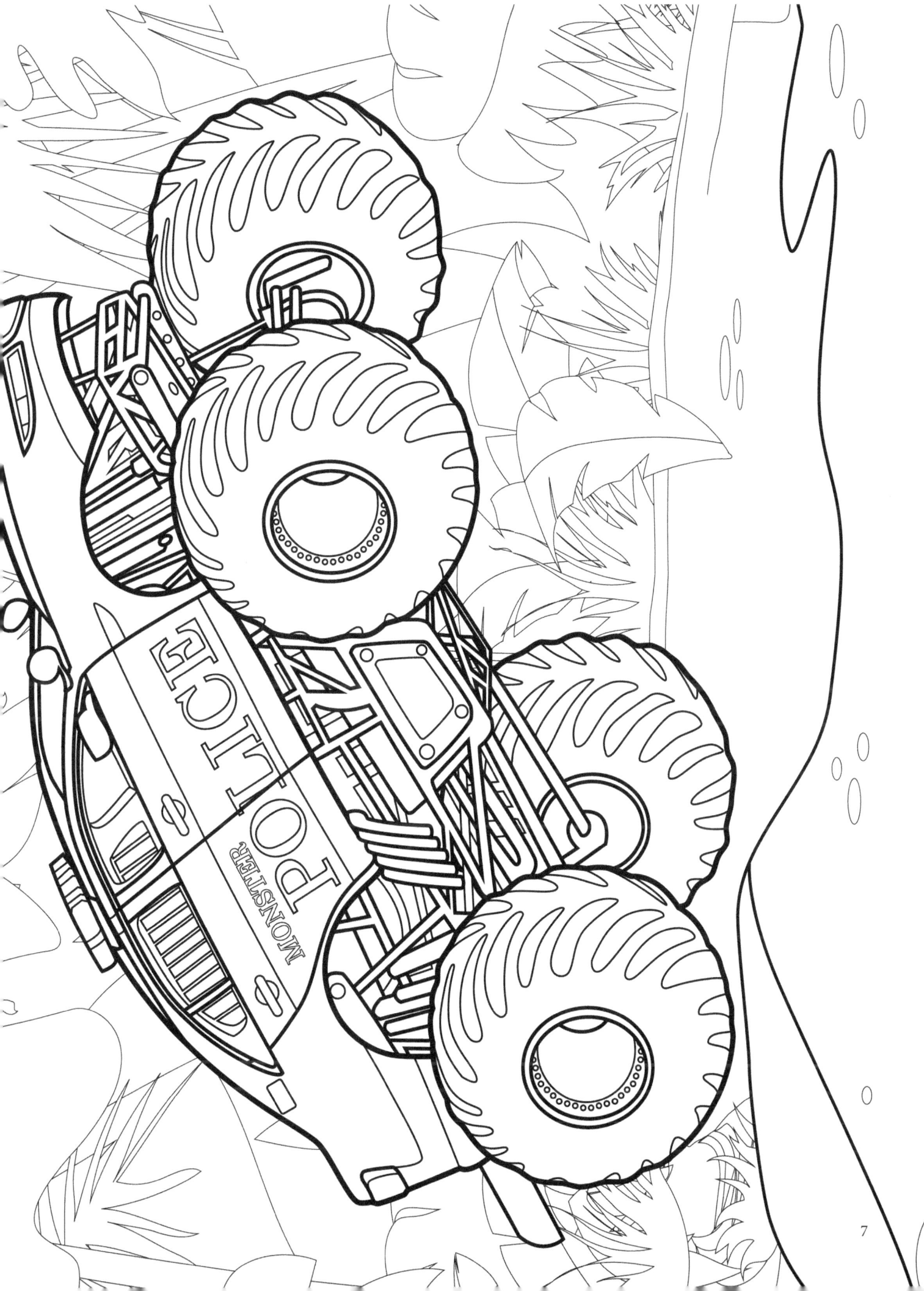

Plate 3.

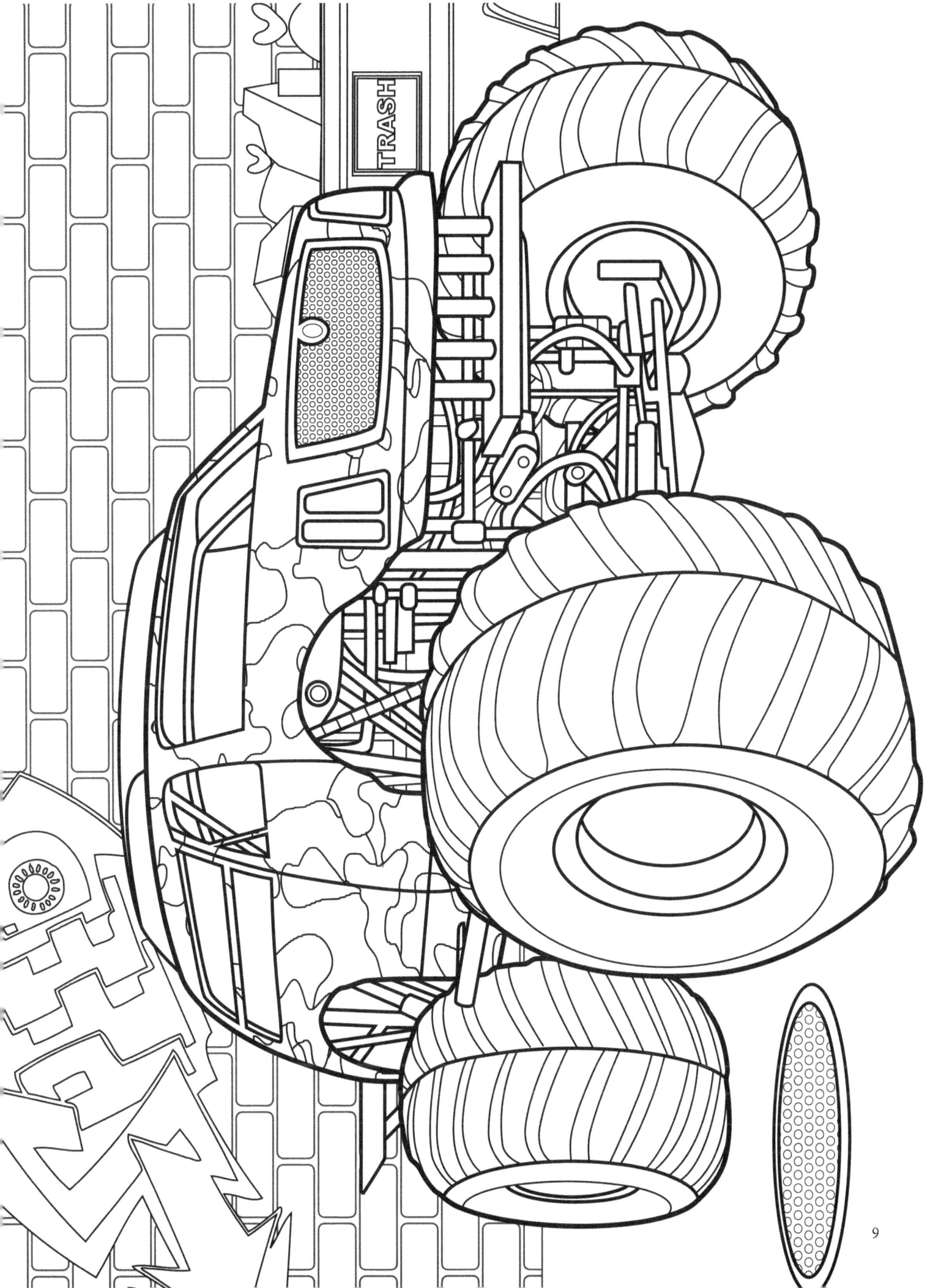

TRASH

9

Plate 4.

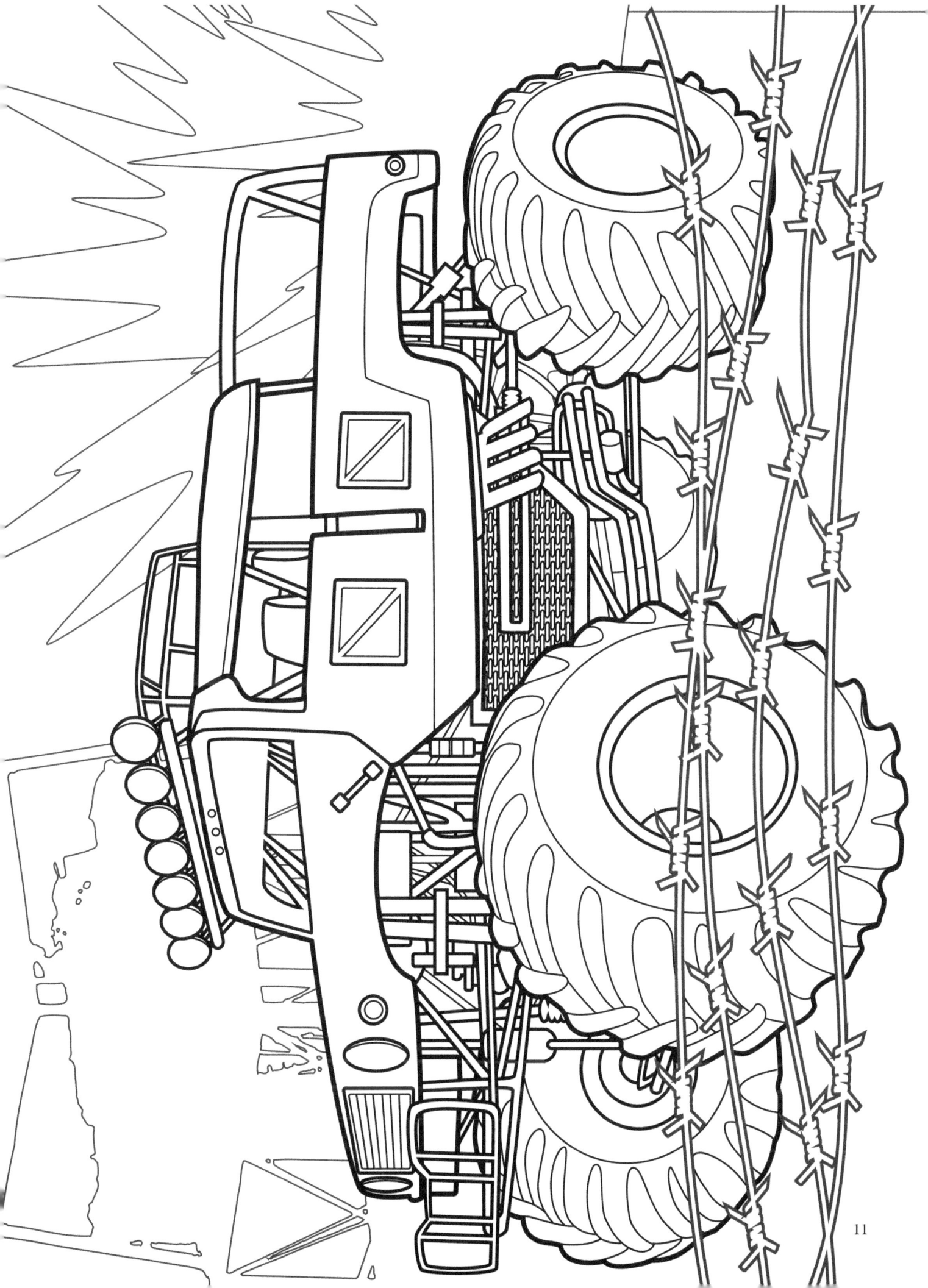

Plate 5.

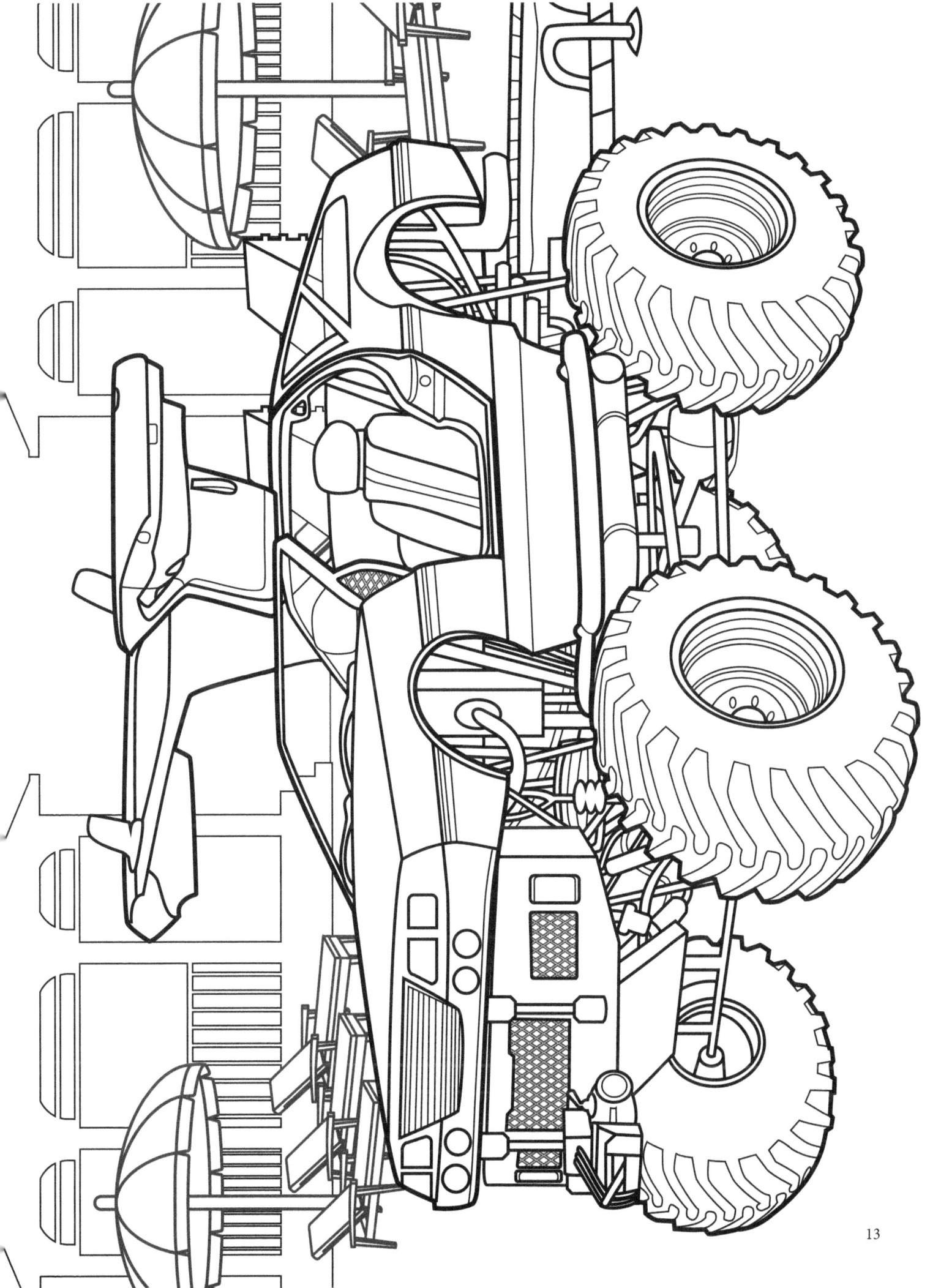

Plate 6.

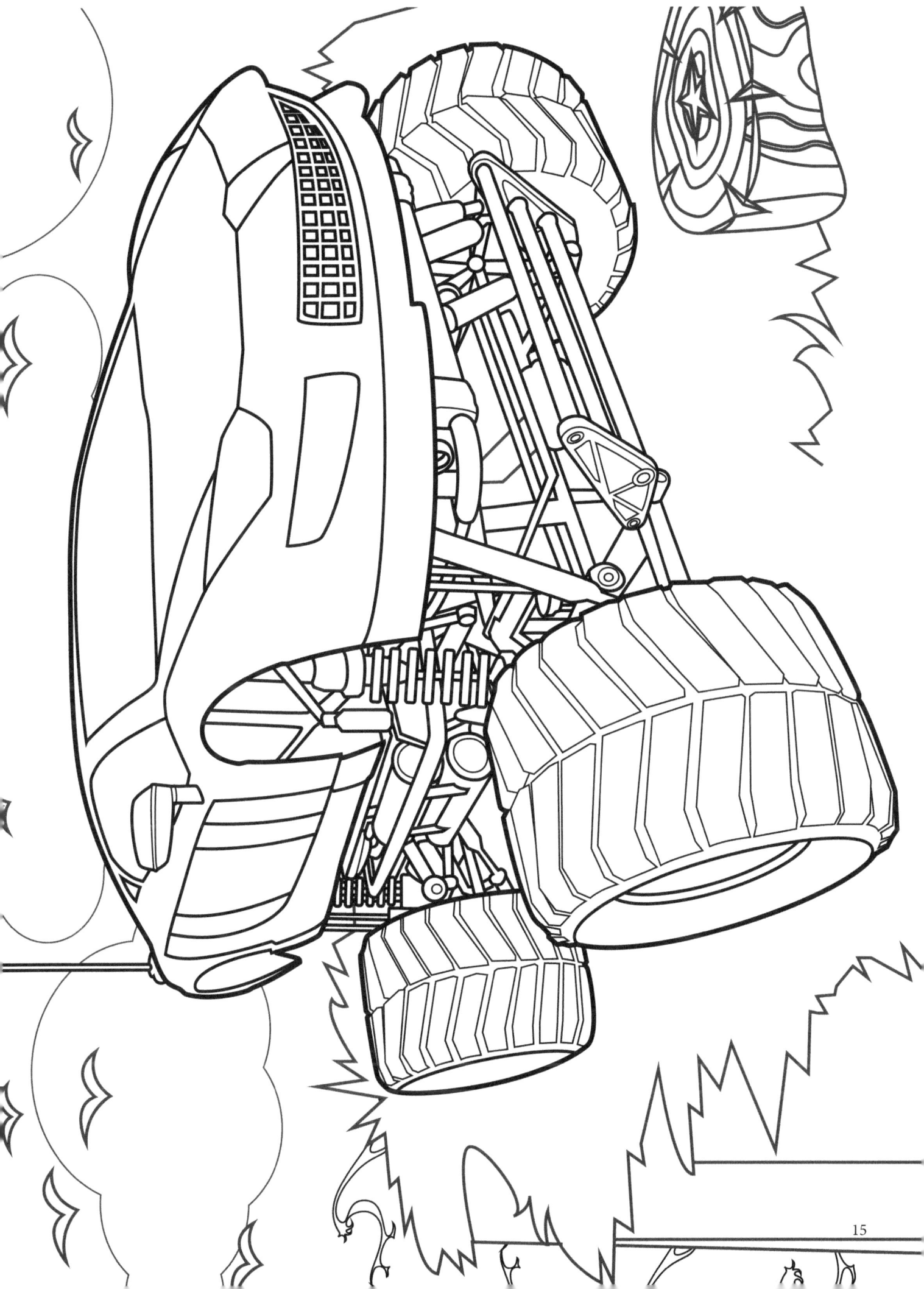

Plate 7.

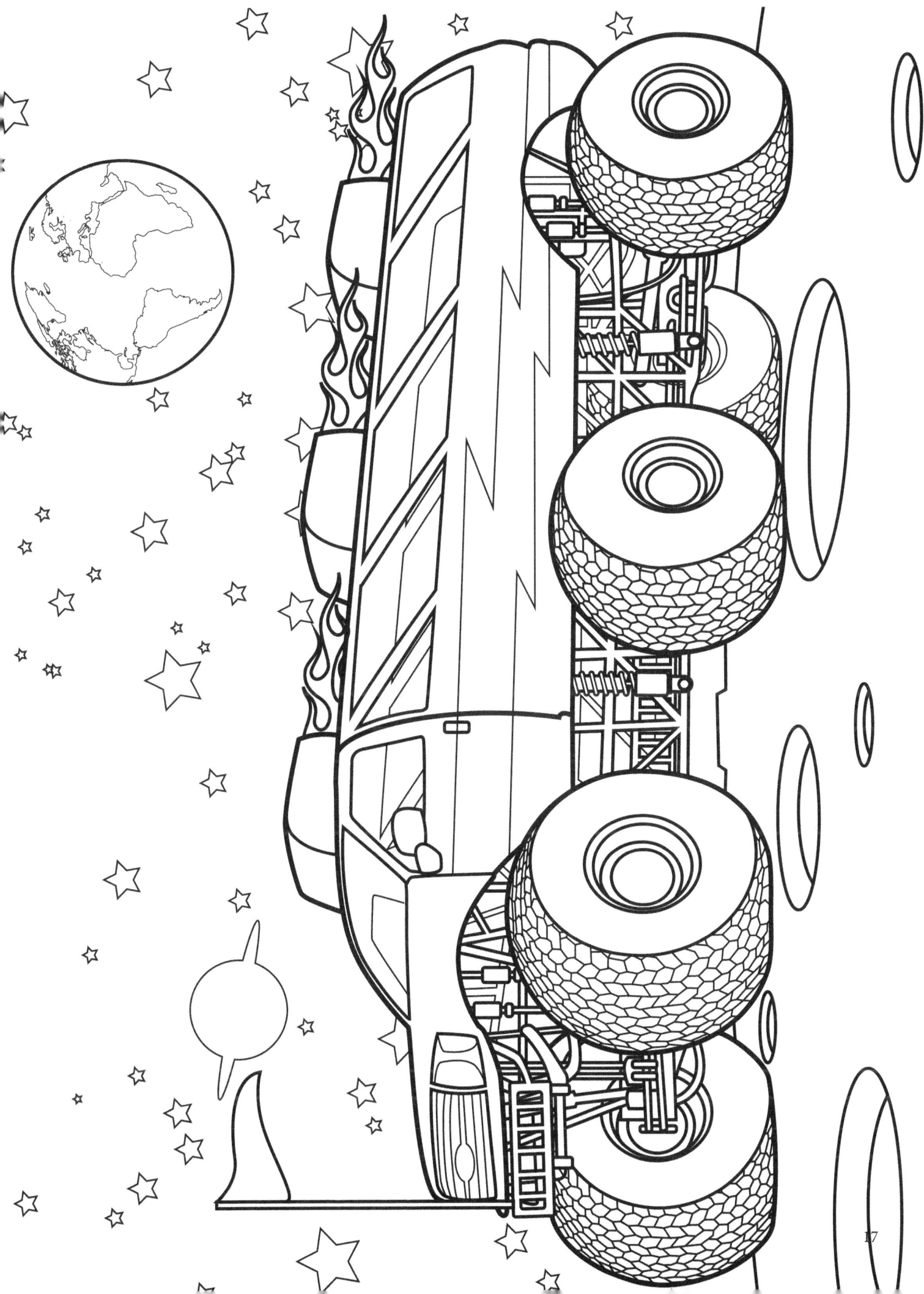

Plate 8.

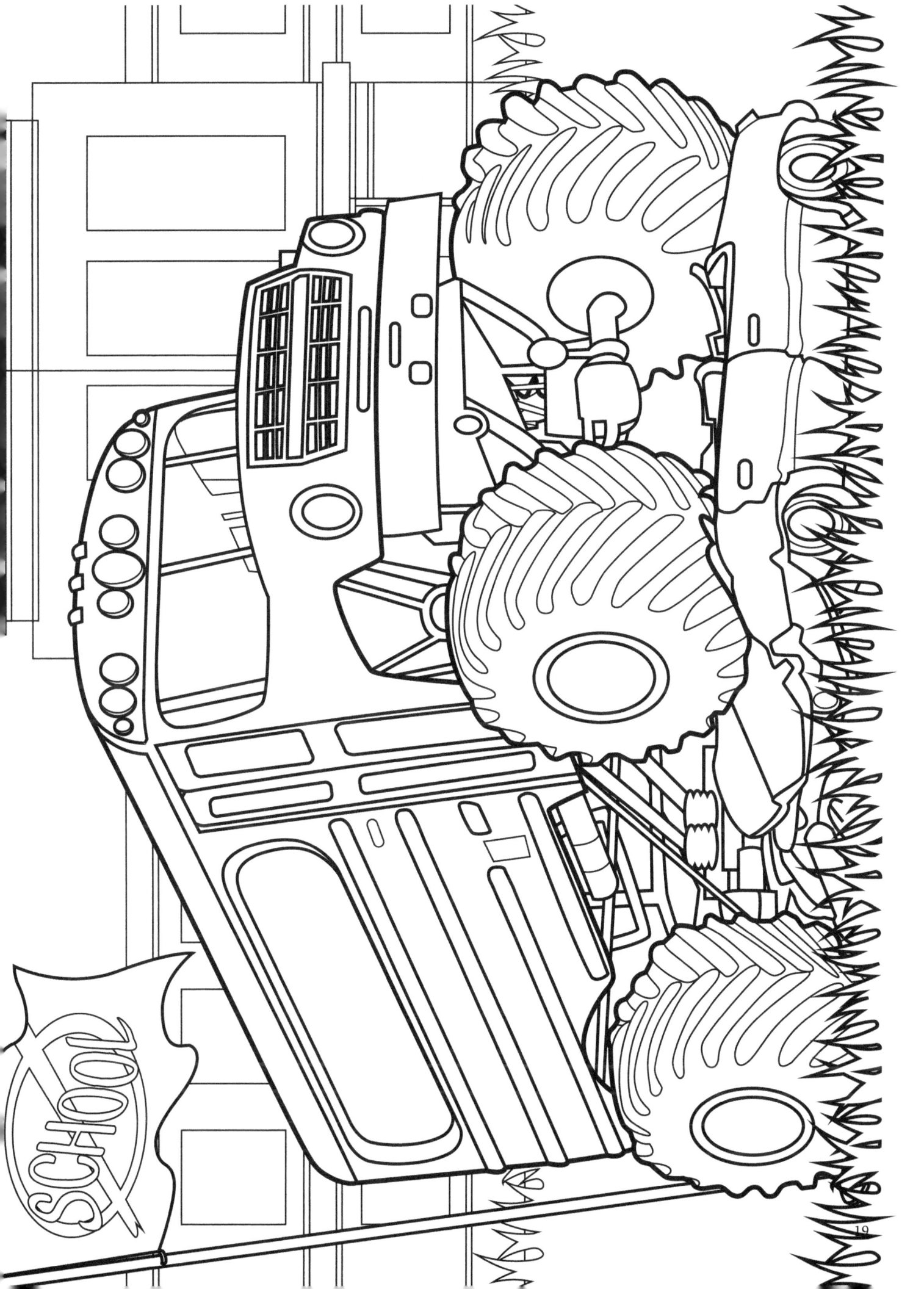

Plate 9.

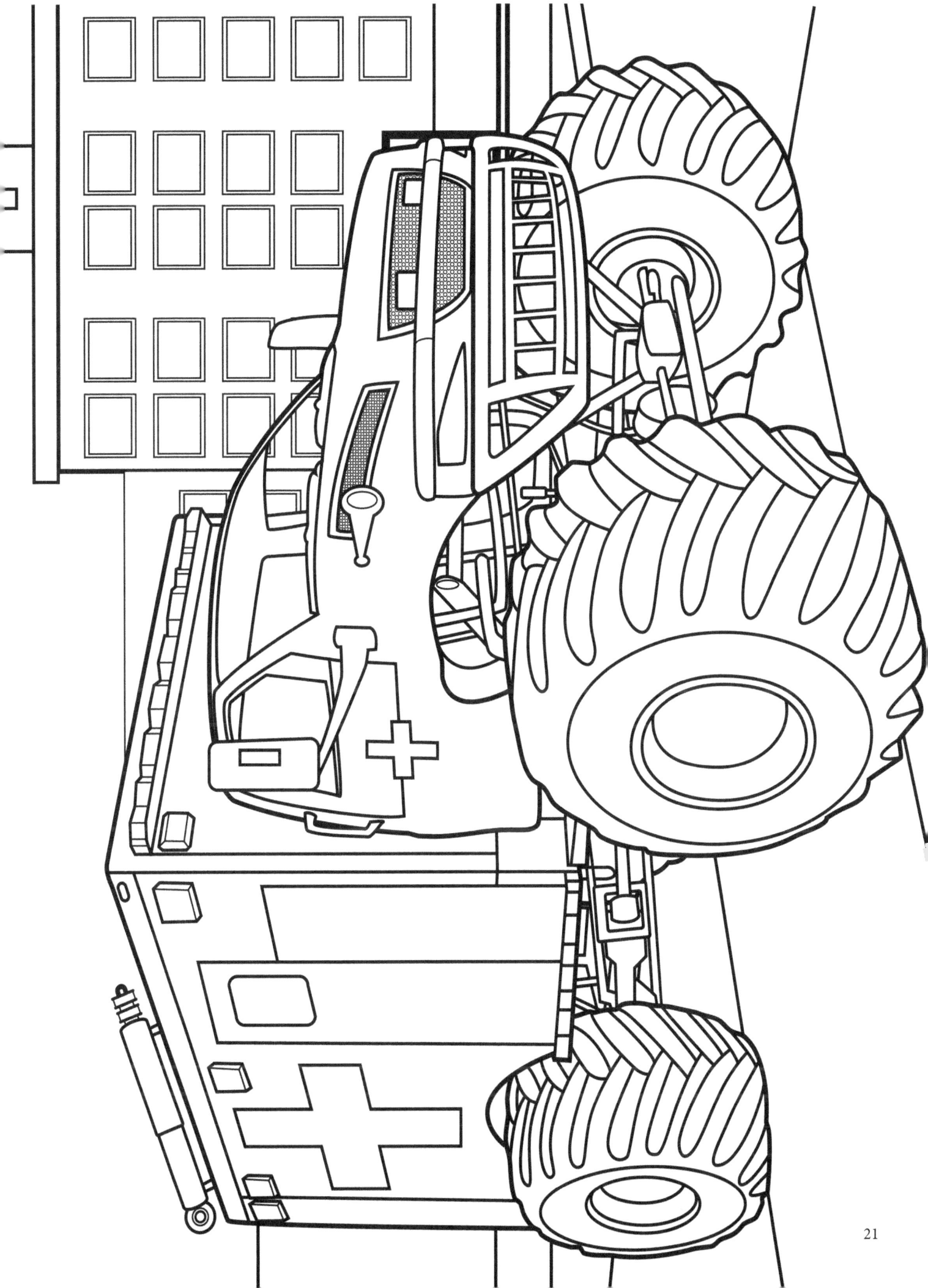

Plate 10.

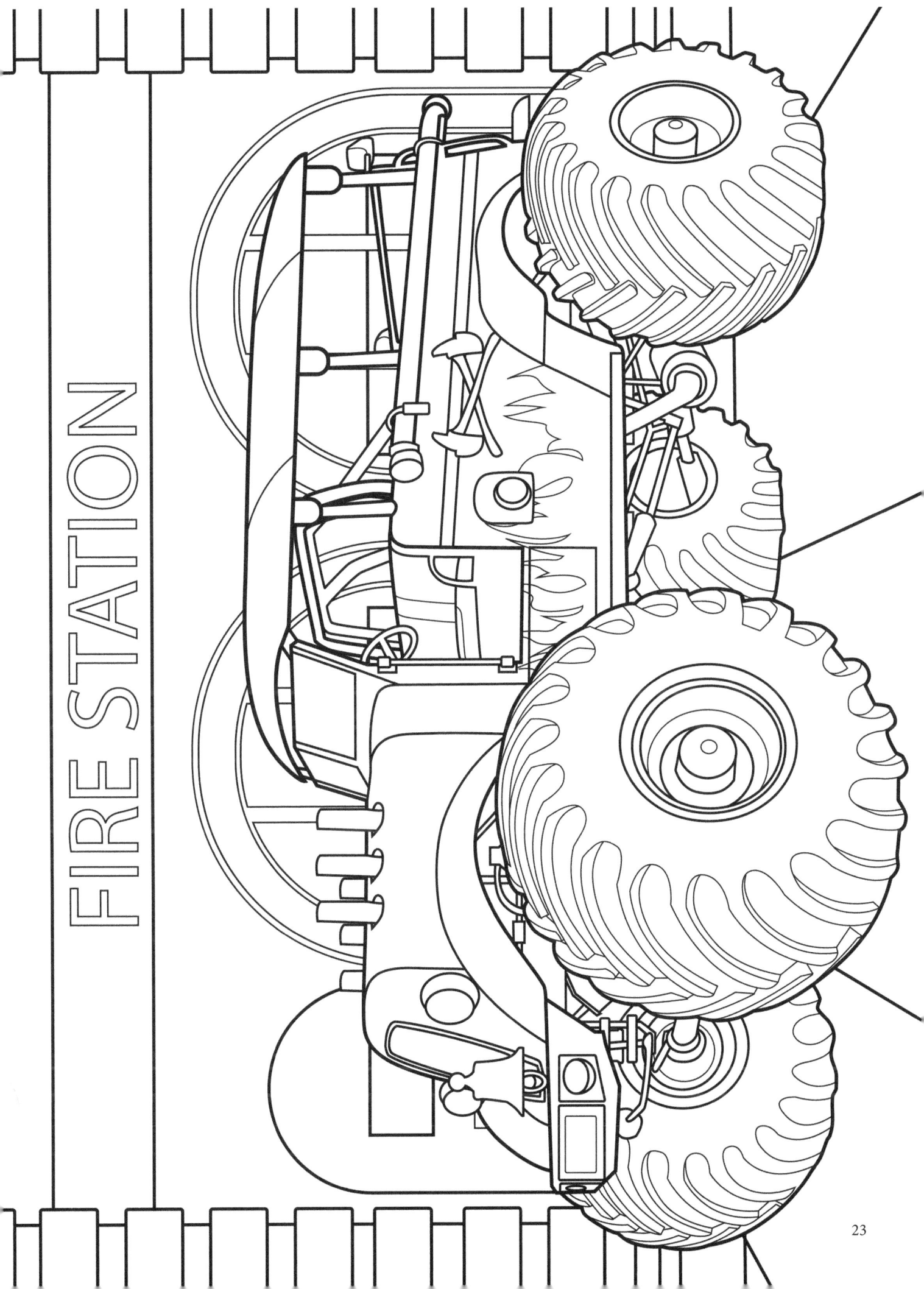

FIRE STATION

23

Plate 11.

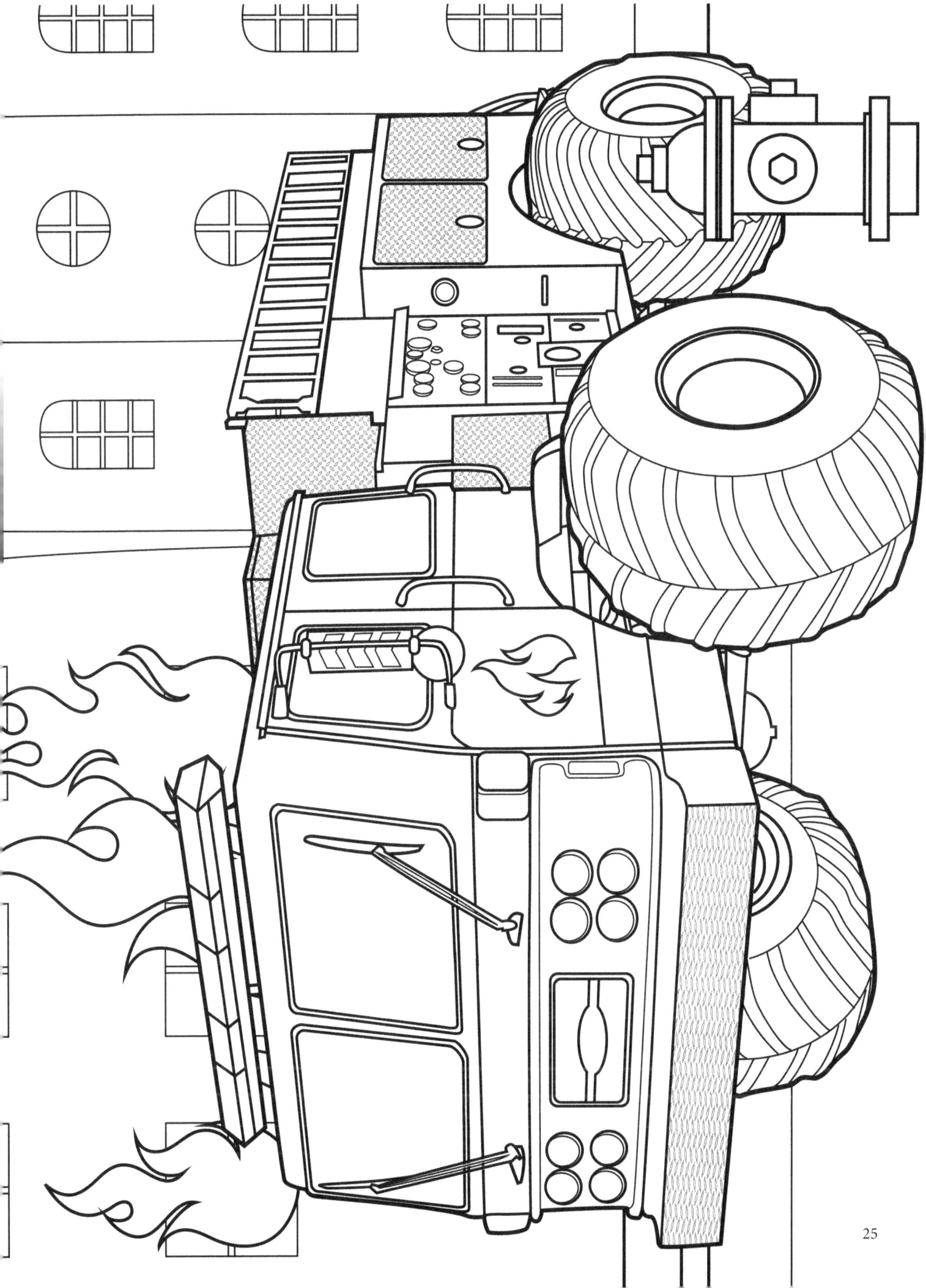

Plate 12.

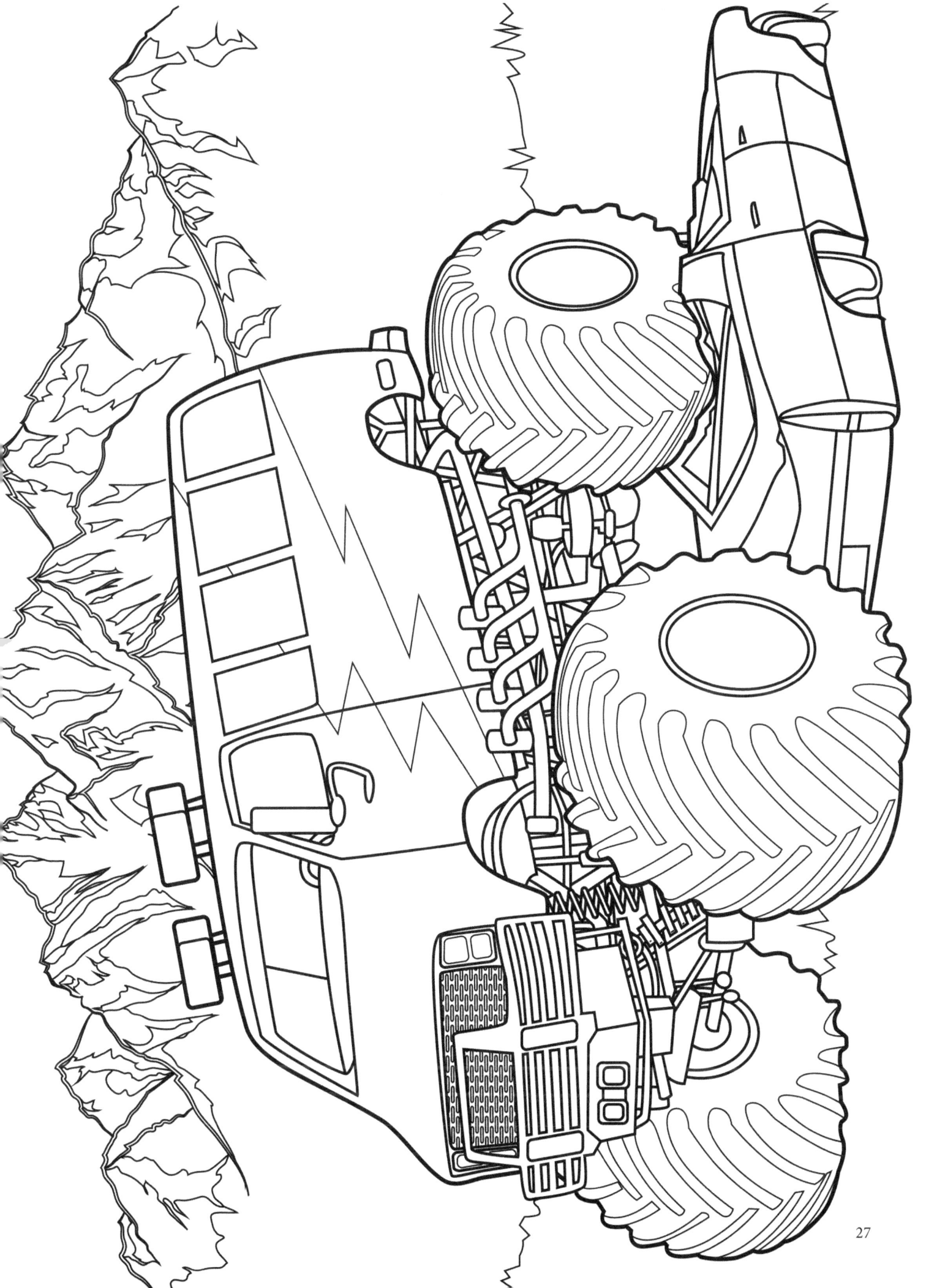

Plate 13.

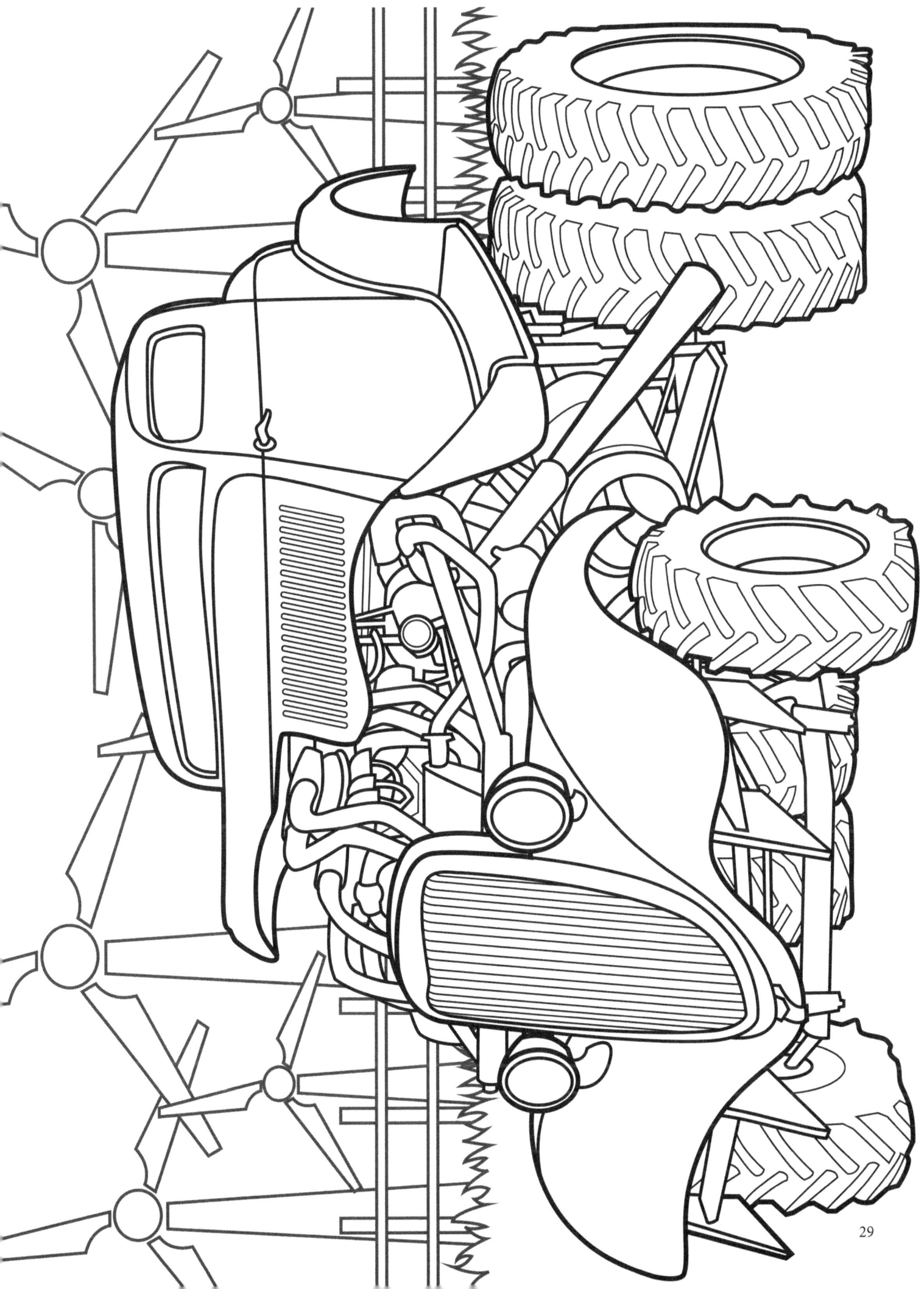

Plate 14.

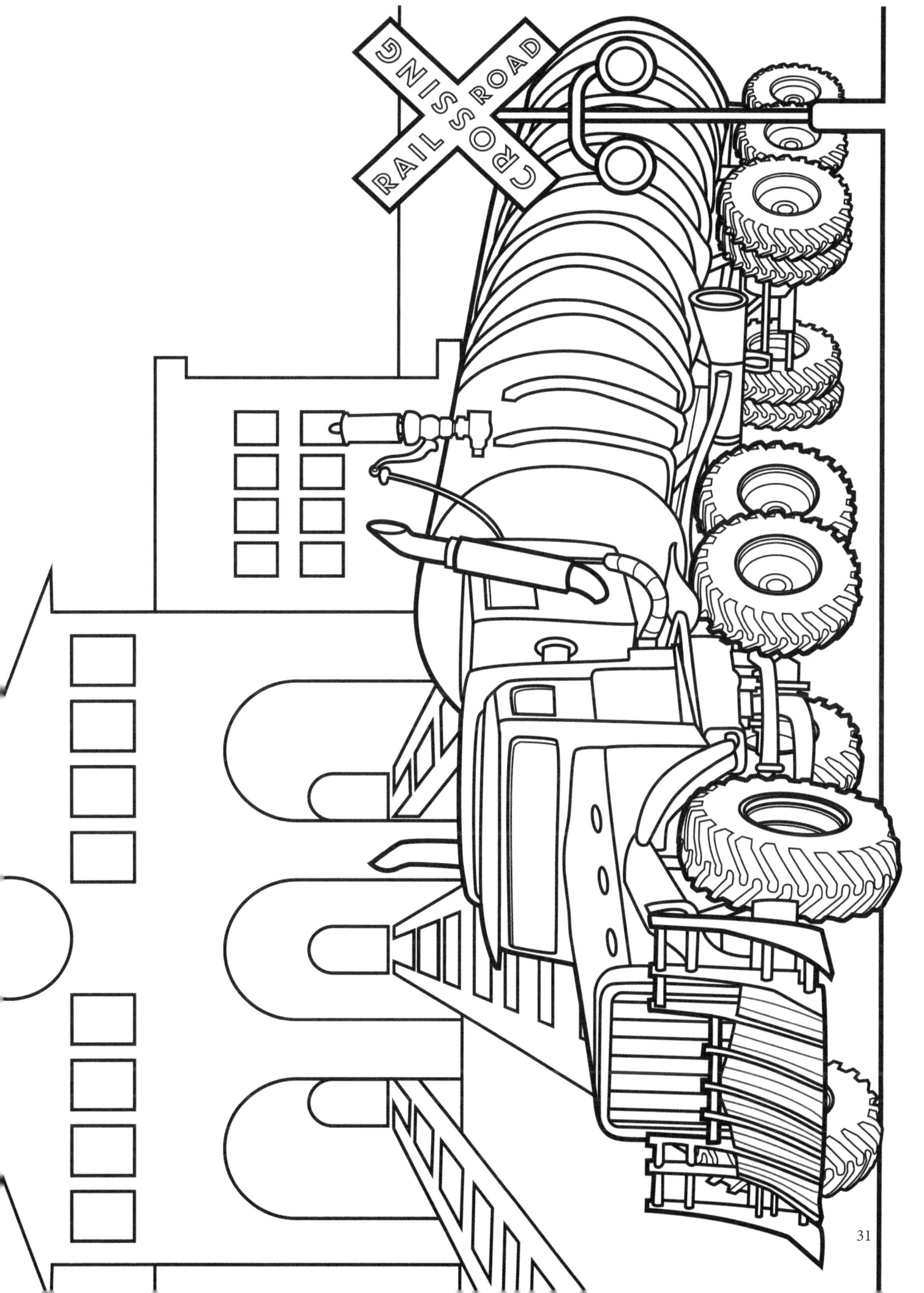

31

Plate 15.

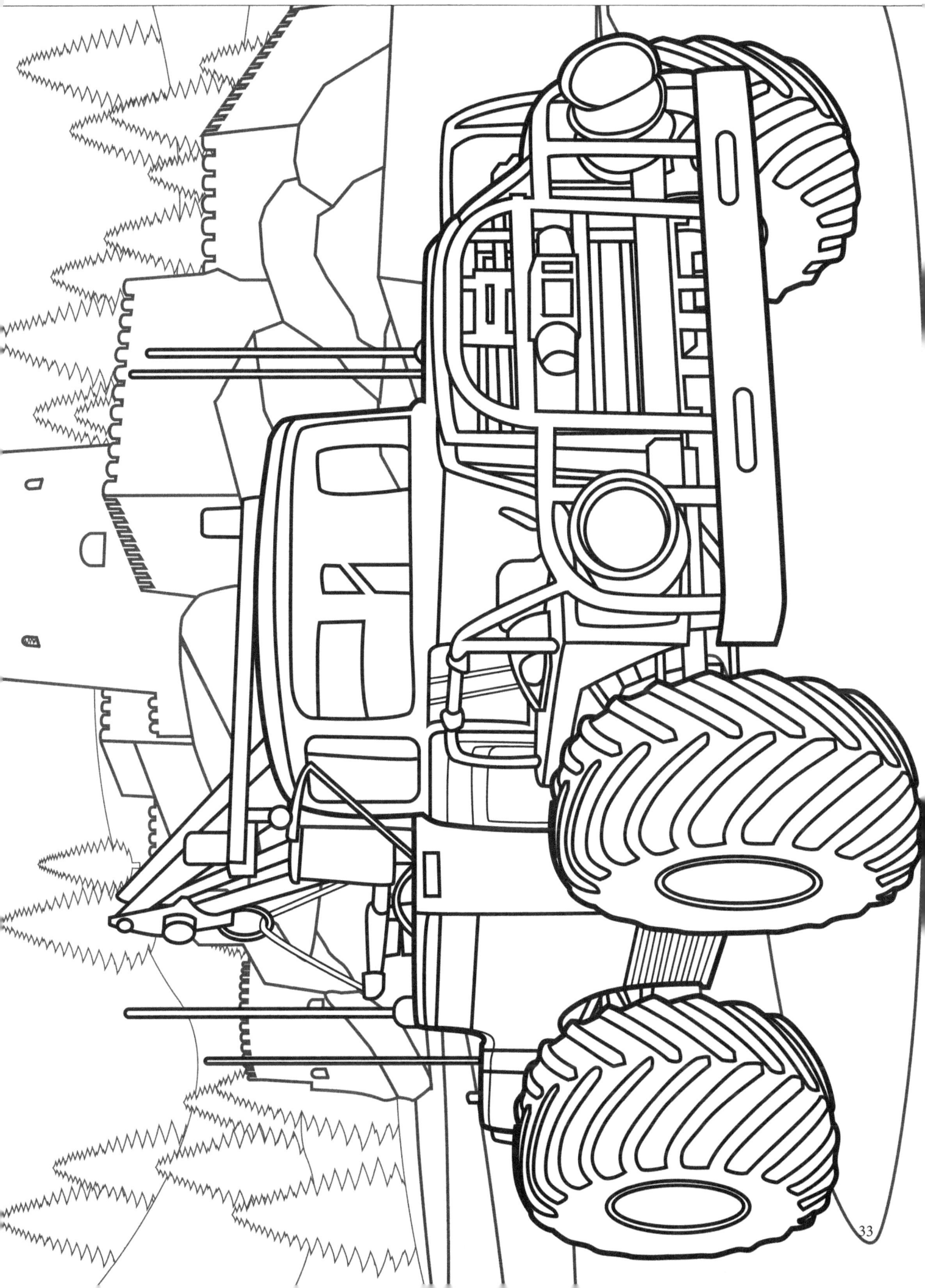

33

Plate 16.

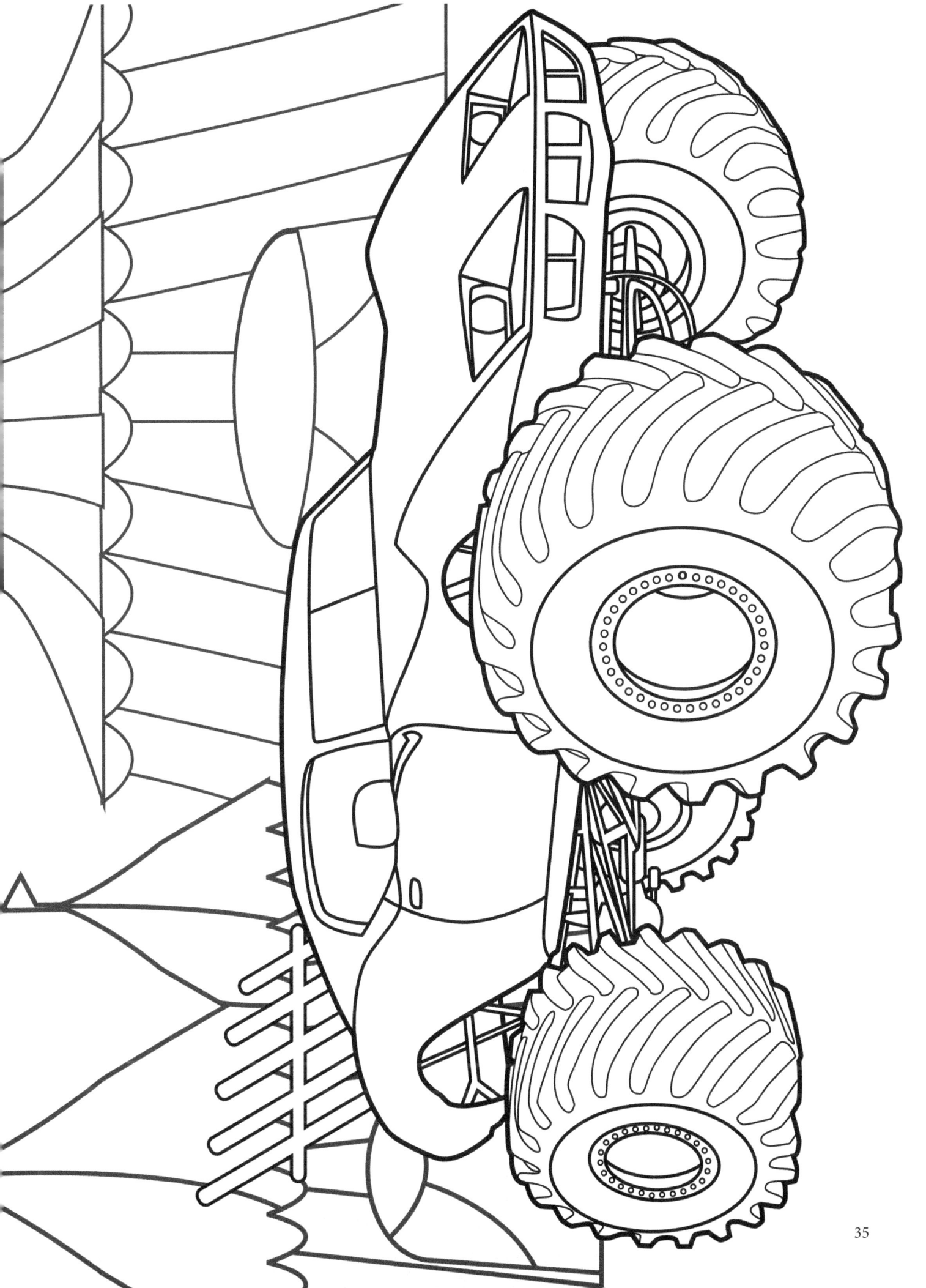

Plate 17.

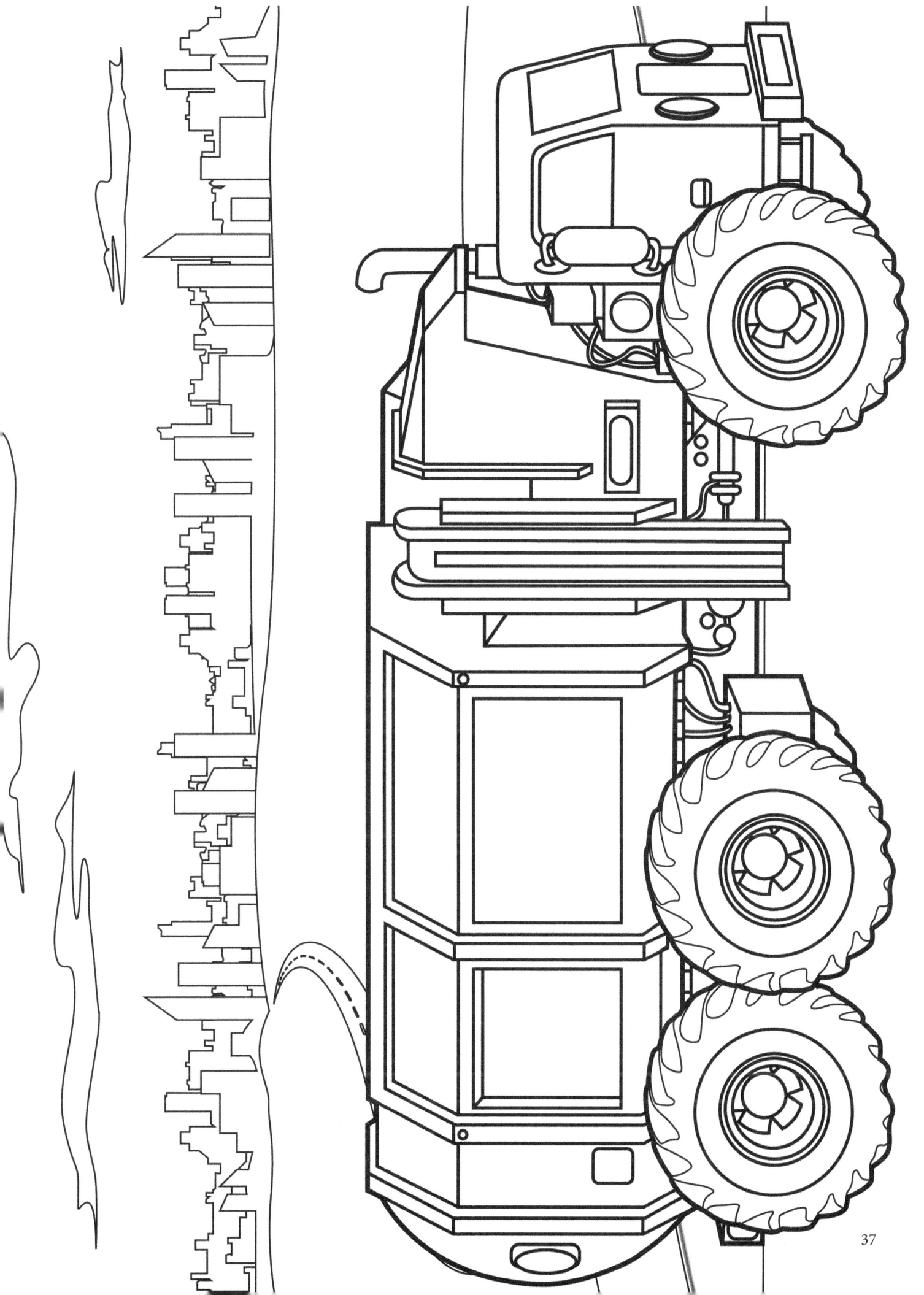

Plate 18.

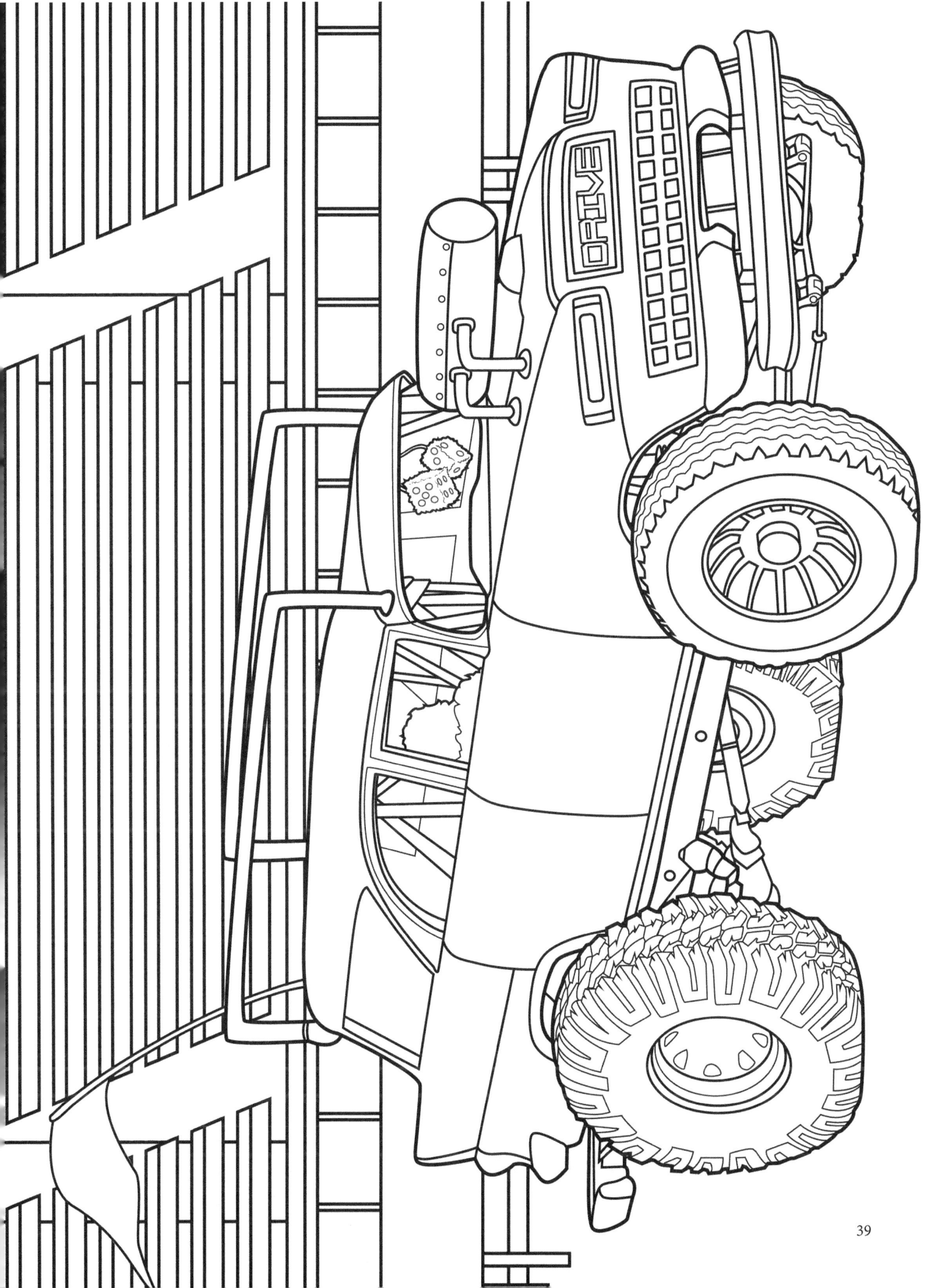

Plate 19.

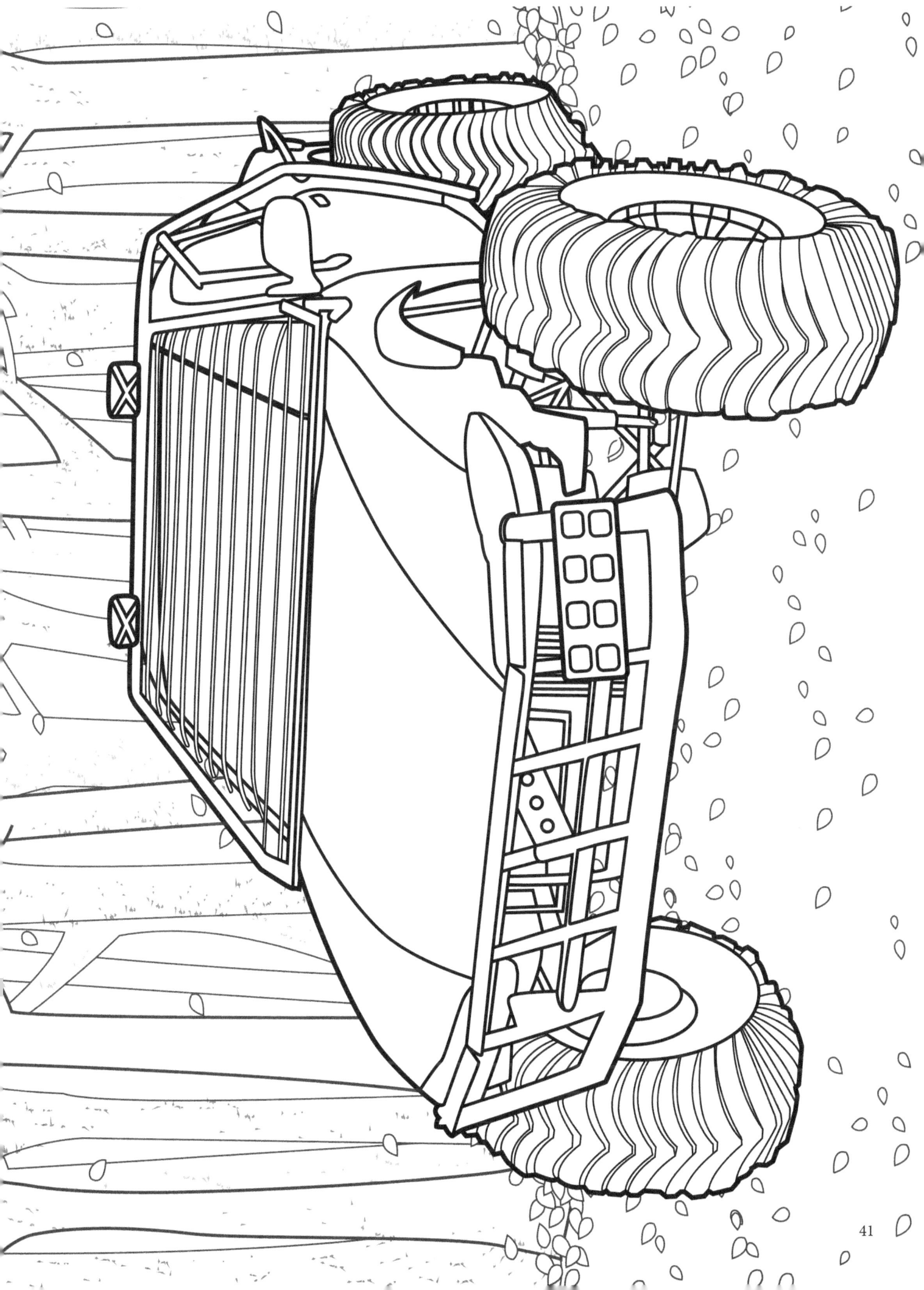

Plate 20.

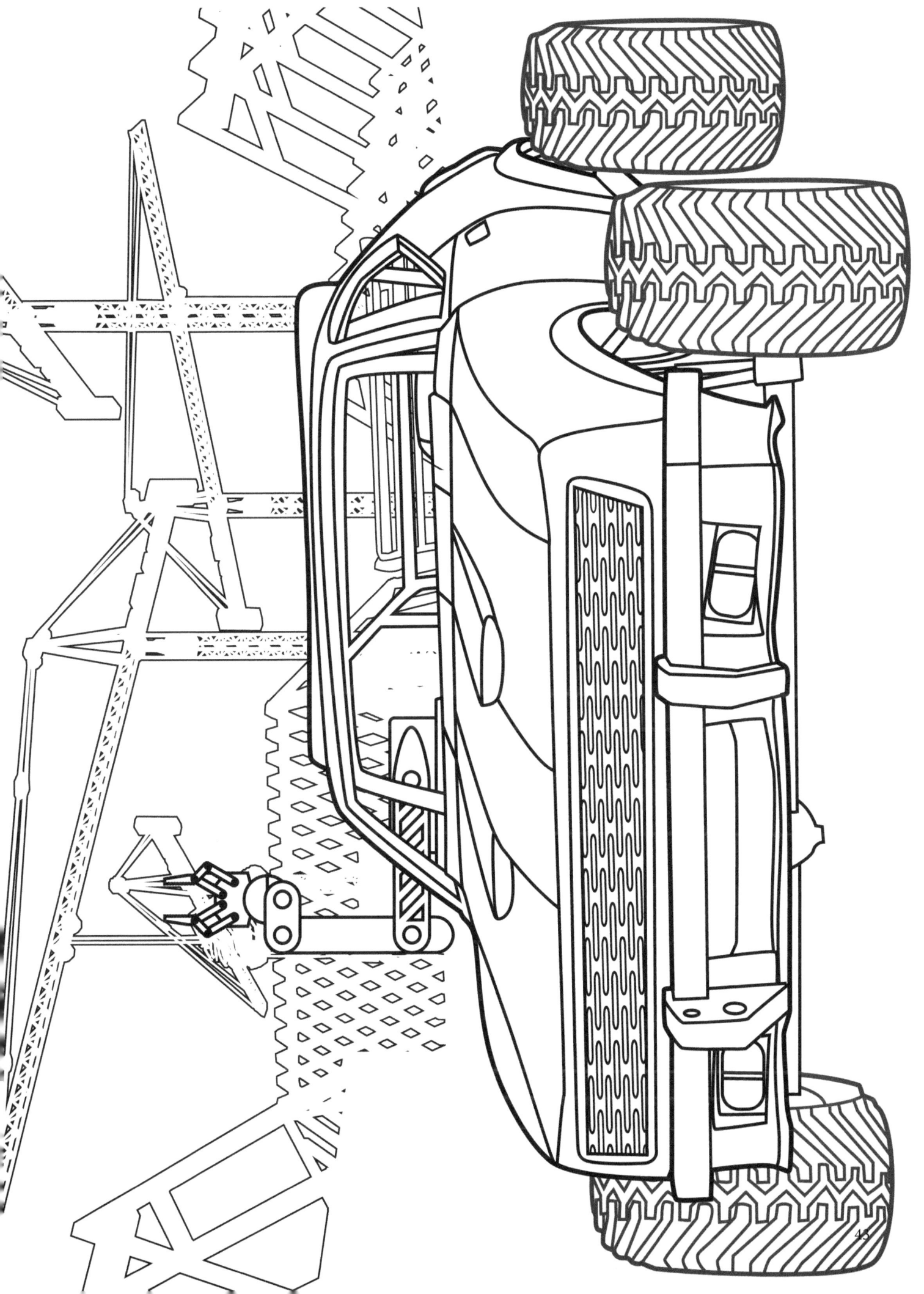

Plate 21.

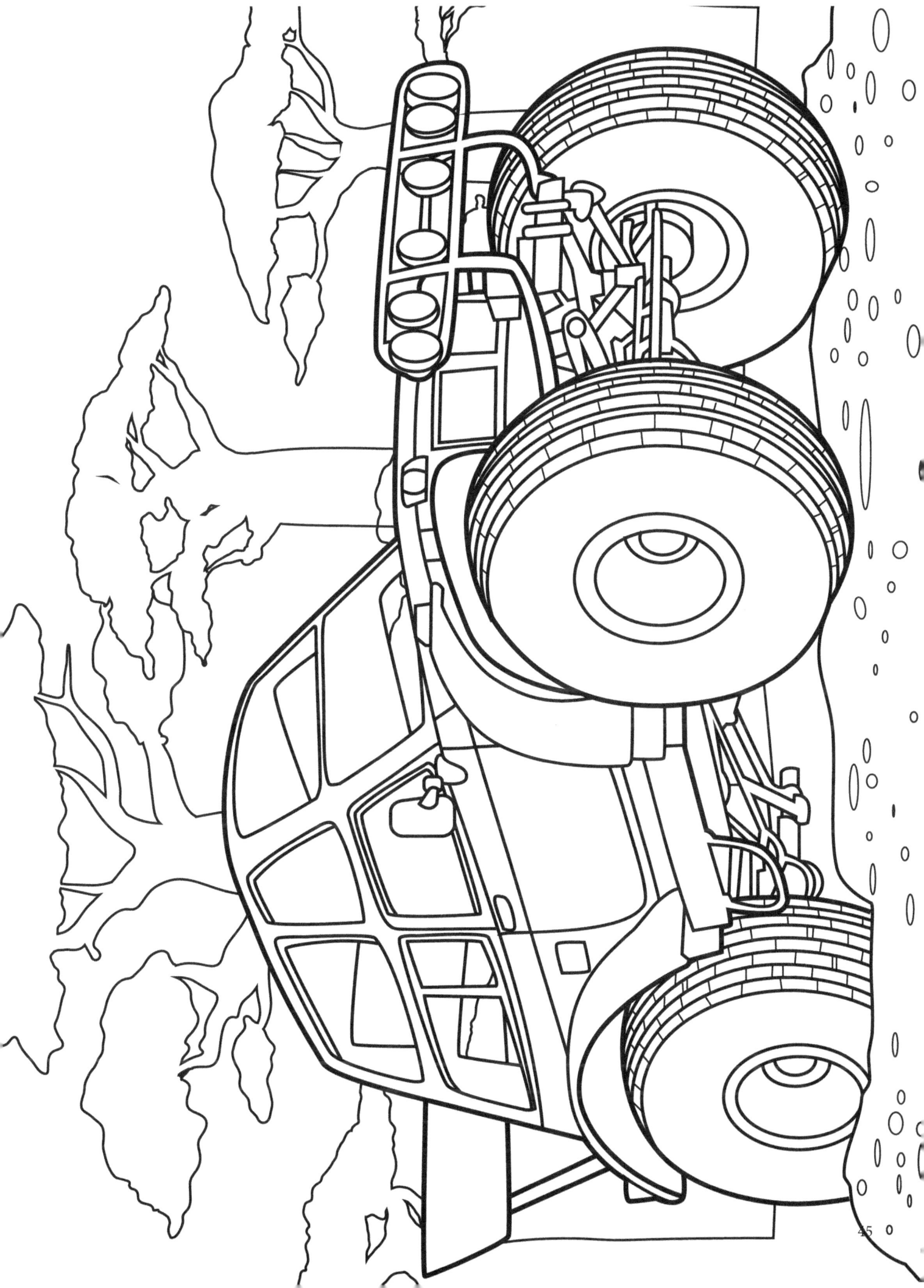

Plate 22.

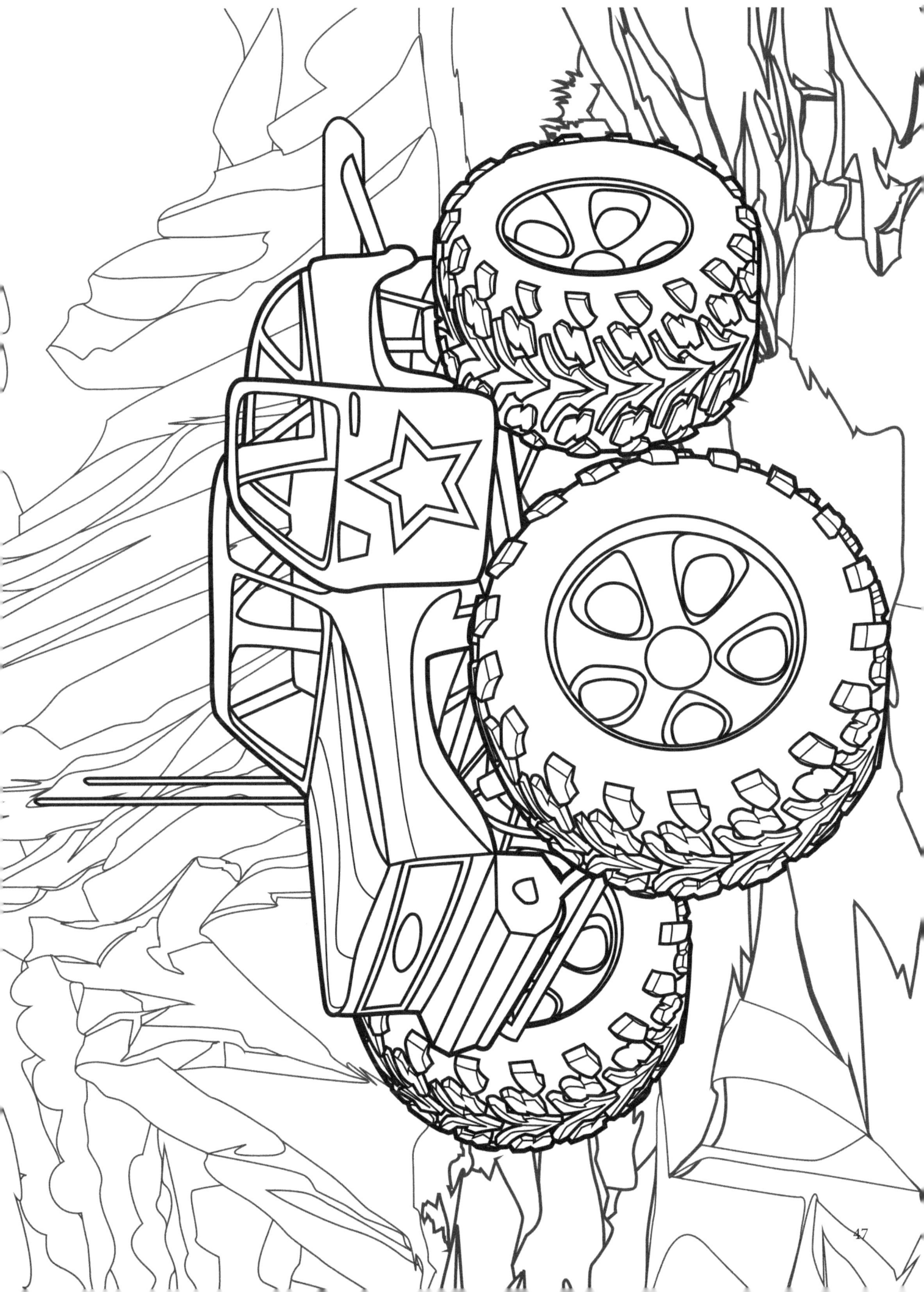

Plate 23.

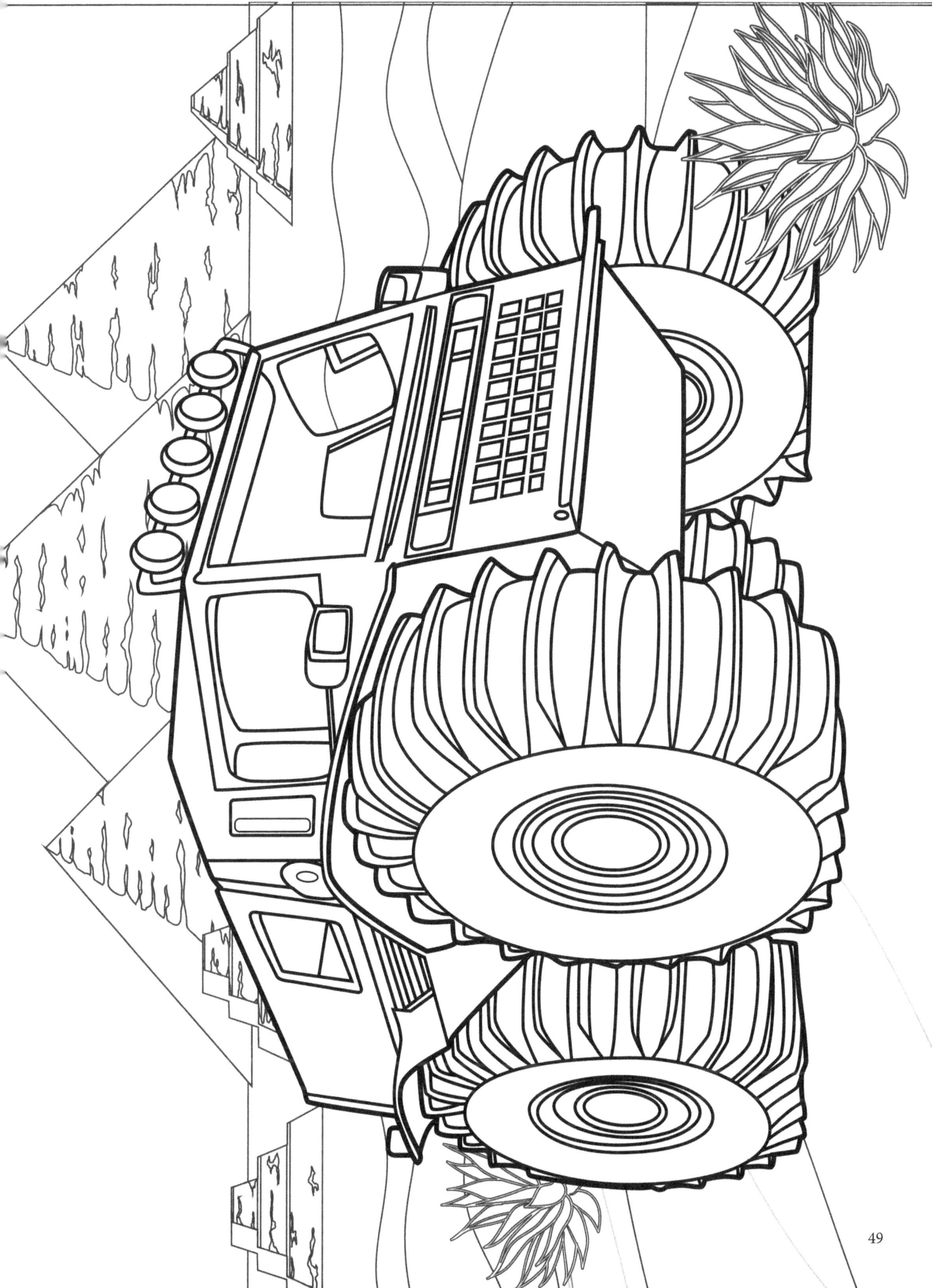

Plate 24.

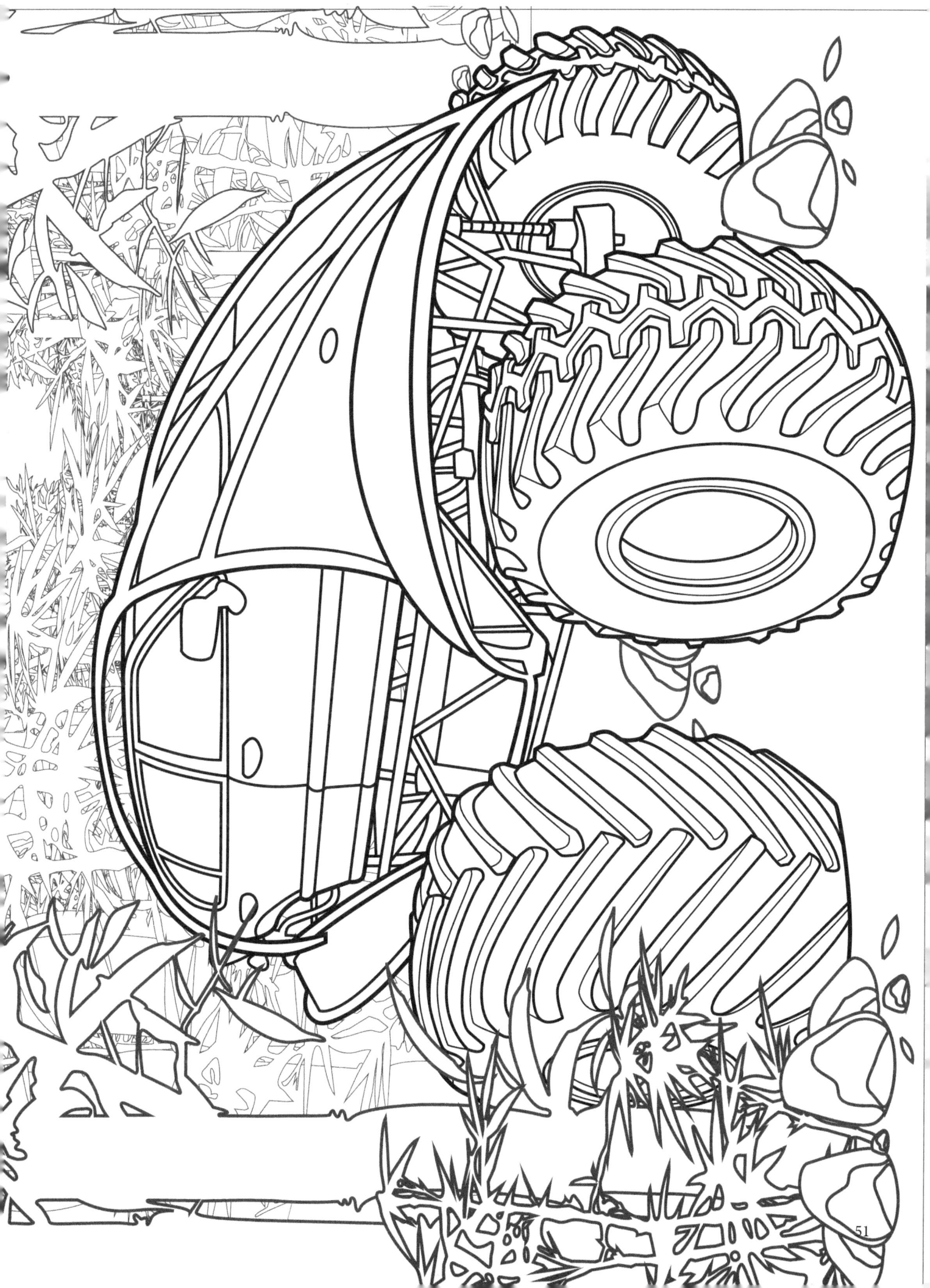

Plate 25.

www.ingramcontent.com/pod-product-compliance
Lightning Source LLC
Chambersburg PA
CBHW081301180526
45170CB00007B/2514